The Run, The Sprint, and The Marathon
by LaMont Reid

Cover Illustration by Victoria Dukuly
Contact: vdukuly6@yahoo.com

Hope Kelley Book Publishing
www.HopeKelleyBookPublishing.
com publish@HopeKelley.com
800.806.6240

Printed in the United States of America

The Run, The Sprint, and The Marathon

by

LaMont Reid

DEDICATION

"I dedicate this writing to my wife, Catrell, for her constant love and support, to my sons Alexander and Kaleb, to my beautiful daughters Kamari and Milan, and to my baby boys Kingston and Morocco. To my mom, Loretta Williams, for everything that I am that is good... your fingerprints are on it. You are all the best reflections of me and God's eternal love through me."

~~ LaMont Reid

TABLE OF CONTENTS

FOREWORD

"I am amazed at the level of revelation that is in this book. *The Run, The Sprint, and The Marathon* is truly a game-changer if you are looking to shift your life toward abundant living. The practical wisdom that is revealed through simple, yet profound truths will open your eyes to the perilous patterns in your life and cause you to alter your direction. Wisdom tells you to get an understanding, and one of the things we must recognize is what is essential and what is non-essential. If we do not understand what is crucial, we will end up wasting our lives on unnecessary things. This book will force you to consider where you have been wasting your life and challenge you to deepen your mind and live your life with new conviction. You will know the truth and the truth will set you free."

~~ Apostle Rob Wallace

PROLOGUE

THIS IS A MUST-READ BOOK!

"The Run, The Sprint, and The Marathon will help you find your pace in life. It is a metaphorical look at the journey of life we all race through.

The book speaks about the cycles in our lives. We are always at one of these stages whether we know it or not, just like a washing machine works to wash, rinse, and then spin. The cycle is an identifier to locate your position and help you to understand what your functionality should be at different phases in life. Sometimes you need to know if you should break the cycle and begin another. This book will give you a direct guide on how to measure a target ten times, but only shoot once. I hope you enjoy reading my book!"

~~ LaMont Reid

CHAPTER 1

The Run

Run! It is a word that is used commonly in our everyday lives. I must make a quick run and then I will return. I hope I do not run into traffic today. My friends are in town, maybe I will run over to them and say hello.

Since I received that disturbing news, my mind has not stop running. I refuse to let people run over me any longer. I have to run downtown for an important meeting. I cannot believe this guy is going to run for president.

As you can see, the word *run* has many different possibilities. We all arrive at the place where we realize we cannot sit still, we cannot walk, wc cannot talk about it anymore. We have to run and run now.

The run is what I like to call the discovery zone, the aha moment, the *I have got it now,* I know what I need to do, let me clear my path because I have work to do. It is the place where we realize we need to hurry up. It is where the sense of urgency consumes us, and we understand we cannot wait any longer and it is time for us to run. We say to ourselves, nothing is going to stop me, no more uncertainty, this is exactly what I should be doing right now.

The first metaphorical application to a good run is things need to be clear and simple. Before you can run there has to be a vision or it should become vision. Anytime you write something down that is not current in your life, even though it will be and can be accomplished. This is the epitome of vision. Habababkuh Ch.2 V. 2 KJV Bible supports this statement.

Write what you envision and make it plain upon tablets. That whoever reads it, may run with it. If there is no vision, running may be hazardous, especially if you plan on running fast.

We have heard and witnessed blind people playing instruments, dancing, reading, employment, participating in events, typing, and accomplishing some spectacular feats. They were able to do these things because although they do not have sight, they do have vision. I have never heard of nor witnessed anyone that was blind running or running fast. There is no way to run without vision.

It must be a frightening thing for a blind person to be forced to run. They have to be totally dependent upon someone else to guide them, although at a much more comfortable pace.

Before anyone can run there has to be vision, not just physical sight, but to the extent that you know why you are running.

Running without a vision, a plan, could have us running in the wrong direction.

Our run could be in vain. We are beginning to understand that sight and vision are not the same. They are vastly different from one another.

Sight gives us the ability to see what is in front of you, while vision gives us the ability to see what will unfold of ahead of us.

Remember this statement. "Sight comes from your eyes, but vision comes from your heart and then released from your mouth."

Sight is great, and I am grateful, and I possess the ability to see. Sight has so many limitations. Even though our eyes are given to us for sight only, we sometimes crave more than what our actual abilities can afford us.

For example, if you walk out of your home and stand in front of your house and turn around and look at your house, the only thing you can see is the house you live in, that is what our sight gives us.

If you walk in front of your house and say,

I like the house I live in, but I will soon have a greater house. What has happened is you have just created vison. The ability to see what is not there but what will be there one day should you pursue the run to get it.
If you focus more on what is in front of you which is sight, it will begin to kill the vision that is inside of you. You will not see.
So now ask yourself this question, are you a Seer or Visionary? A Seer can always see what is in front of them, but a Visionary always sees what is before them and what lies ahead. The Seer will have a different mindset from the Visionary. I am willing to bet the character of a seer will be someone who is very up and down emotionally, physically, moody, pessimistic, double minded, inconsistent, fault finding, and full of frustration.

But the character of the visionary will be someone who is cheerful, hopeful, diligent, patient, full of gratitude, and pays attention to the smallest of details. I can speak for myself. I have been a Seer for such a long time, but now I am a Visionary. Do not get me wrong, there are times where I have reverted and went back to being a Seer.

In a race, you have to decide early on that you are going to win. It cannot just be a thought, but it must be a declaration. Desire is not enough on its own, there are many people that want but still lack.

There are many different reasons that people *physically* run. Some people run because they enjoy exercising, some run because they need to exercise, and others may run because they enjoy the solitude and peace that one can obtain while running.

Some may run because something or someone could be chasing them. Others may run because they have something to prove or disprove. There are plenty of people that run just to relieve stress and anxiety. No matter what the motivation, they do it as it seems important to do so. It seems to me that running is very well respected.

The one thing amongst many that I respect about running is people usually have the tendency to get out of your way. My definition of run is to move faster than your normal pace.

Running is usually coupled with a purpose, not many people run for no reason. I apologize for that statement because kids run all the time for no reason at all, but you get my point!

Running can be a defense or an offense, it all depends on how it is being used when needed. In the animal world, If, it is a cheetah running its being used as an offense, but if it is a gazelle, it's a defense.

Both animals use running as a means for survival. Their very lives are dependent on their ability to run. If the cheetah does not run, they do not eat. Their ability to hunt is gripped in their running. If the gazelle does not run, it is in peril because it possesses no other defense to protect itself.

The cheetah is considered one of the small cats in the wild. However, they are capable of taking down prey that are three times their size. They are not as large as other big cats such as the lion, tiger, jaguar, leopard, or cougar. But the lion turns away from no adversary and possesses an intimidating roar.

The cheetah is known to retreat and roars so lightly that it could be mistaken for a bird's chirp. The tiger is the largest cat species, which has the size to overpower its prey and opponents. The cheetah is lightly built and mostly hunts in the daytime.

This makes perfect sense because other big cats hunt at night.

But the cheetah is so fast that it has been known to run up to 70 to 85 mph, and if it is going to run that fast, the daytime would probably be the best time to do it.

The jaguar is the third largest cat. It has an exceptionally powerful bite. It normally targets the skull of its prey and bites straight through. The cheetah uses a tripping tactic and suffocates it prey. The leopard has short legs and a long body with a large skull. The cheetah has an exceedingly small head and slender body. The cougar is secretive and largely solitary by nature, while the male cheetah is known to form groups to hunt.

I intentionally brought out the comparison of the cheetah to other big cats not to show

how insignificant the cheetah is, or how it does not even measure up as far as strength, power, or dominance, but to point out that we spend too much time comparing who we are to what we are not. The cheetah is not made for strength, nor is it made for power or sophistication. It is built simply for the run. Knowing who you are is equally important as knowing who you are not.

That is why you will not find people who suffer with identity crisis, low self-esteem, or a poor self-image achieve great levels of success. Although, in some cases there is always an exception to the rule.

Success should be your own personal mark, not the mark others have set for you. There is a lesson to be learned from the cheetah. The cheetah is not the lion, tiger, leopard, jaguar, or cougar, and neither is it trying to be. Embrace who you are. Knowing who and what you are, is the beginning of discovering where your strength and dominant talents reside. As we venture through life we work hard to find out where we fit in. But while we work to find that place or group of people, we need to concentrate on the area that makes us different from everyone else. We are designed in a particular way for a reason, If the cheetah tried being any other big cat than what it was made to be, it would not be the fastest land animal in the world.

Embracing who you are, what you are and why you are, automatically makes anyone number one! When most people are not sure of who they are, they work hard to blend in and demand attention.

But, when you know who you are, without effort you stand out and command attention. Cheetahs are recognized even when there not running.

Our world is filled with people who do not want to embrace who they are, what they are or what they were made to be by design. There is a tendency to create what would be more likable and acceptable in the minds of themselves as opposed to what is true. How can it be that animals are unwilling to go against their true nature but we as human beings think we can go against our nature? Can you imagine if a sheep did not want to be a sheep anymore and decided to go into a wolf pack for acceptance? The wolves would welcome the sheep but, they would not embrace the sheep as a wolf. The sheep is prey in the eyes of a wolf no matter how the sheep sees itself. In the animal kingdom the evaluations are quite different from humans. Animals base a great percentage of judgements on their ability to smell. If a sheep could change their outer appearance to be accepted by wolves it would still be a failed attempt. No matter how much a sheep could disguise itself it could not produce the natural smell of a wolf.

Wolves sense of smell reveals to them everything they need to know. If they need to attack or sometimes it takes them a while to determine what the issue is because it can be an unfamiliar smell. Even when animals are going to mate, they make sure that they smell the potential mate's urine to determine that they are not of the same bloodline. If they figure out, they are of the same bloodline they run in the other direction. Animal instincts should not outweigh human intelligence. They should not be able to pick more suitable mates than human beings. Why do we as humans not apply the same resolve when we are determining potential mates? If we are not producing the same thing, why do we not run in the other direction? In the scenario that I just gave about the sheep and the pack of wolves. Let us just say for instance, the sheep does not want to be a sheep. It tries to deny its own nature and attempts to be embraced by the pack of wolves as a wolf. The wolves attack him, and he immediately retreats.

The sheep gets away but discovers that he has been wounded from countless bites in his flesh from the wolves. The sheep does not have a shepherd to patch up his wounds and nurse him back to health. This is in the wild, there are no doctors available. Now the sheep is in more danger than what he was initially. Remember I said that animals rely heavily on their sense of smell. If any animal is in the wilderness and they are bleeding. They can be considered as prey. Even though the sheep was able to get away from the wolves. The only animals they are going to attract are predators. When the scent of blood is in the air, it will attract all the predators on the land. Not only will the predators be alerted, but it will also be the predators of the air; such as eagles, buzzards, crows etc. This is what happens in the animal world. What happens in our human world is remarkably similar. When a human being has been scarred, wounded, neglected, abandoned and they have not been healed from the trauma they experienced, they too will alert predators of the land and predators of the air. The predators of the land will be sent in human form disguised as new potential friendships-relationships.

Be careful since they can sometime be disguised right in your family tree. The new interest is being sent by the predators of air which are demon powers. The powers move on the emotions and mental state of those with open wounds. The sheep has commanded so much attention now because they were not willing to embrace their nature. Of course, this story is contrived in the wild. Animals do not usually go against their nature.

Human beings, on the other hand, will and have done so. This sheep and wolf example are so parallel to life itself because wounds, scars, and a lack of purpose will attract predators into your life. Men and women hear this clearly if you have wounds, bruises, scars, and a lack of purpose. Run, go get healed and nurse yourself back to health and to wholeness because if you do not, you are only going to attract predators. People who will be attracted to you for your weaknesses not your strengths. Running requires for an individual to be in top physical shape. If there is a cut, bruise, scar, tear, or bleeding, you are not equipped to be running. The race has its difficulties and challenges built into it.

It will not be beneficial to carry unnecessary weights that will only slow you down and prevent you from producing maximum performance.

Although many individuals can and have run with various deficits in a race and in life circumstances. But it is not the recommended way we should be running. Everything in your body and on your body must cooperate if you are going to be a runner. There must be complete harmony in the sense that every mechanism of the body is doing its part. Maybe you like me have heard the saying do not major in minors, well that saying does not apply here.

The smallest infraction can be detrimental in a race. A runner will make sure their shoes are suitable for their feet. Also, that their clothes are light enough and they do not carry any excess weight. I run with my cell phone all the time and let me tell you it is a huge inconvenience at times no matter how I place it inside of my band.

The cell phone becomes an unnecessary but necessary weight that I wish I did not have to carry. It is a compass that is a great assistant for my run.

One day I remember watching the Animal Planet on television one and it was showing the Big Cat Diaries. I have always been fascinated with the big cats such as the lion, cheetah, tiger, cougar, and the leopard. Their daily habits have always sparked my interest.

As I began watching the cameramen on a tv show, there was a whole pride of lions that they were following. If you are not familiar with the phrase *pride of lions,* it is just a family of lions. There were as many as fifteen. There were about seven adult females, two half-grown males, and about six cubs. They were watching the pride for about a couple days and two of the cubs got lost in the tall grass. The cameraman and his crew were overly concerned about the cubs being lost. So, the camera men decided to separate. One camera man kept up with the pride of lions while the others followed the two lost cubs.

The cameramen that were watching the two lost cubs were afraid for the danger that awaited those cubs. Those baby cubs were very unaware of the predators that would devour them if they were discovered.

As the program went on the camera man became conflicted because he wanted to rescue those cubs but did not want to interrupt the true nature of the wild. Therefore, he got a handle on his emotions and did not get involved.

As they began to observe these two cubs, all at once a herd of buffalo began to run where the cubs were. As the buffalo began to run violently, one of the cubs was killed, leaving just one cub to navigate in the wild all alone. After that incident they named the other cub Lucky because it should have been killed like the other.

It became pretty clear what would be the destiny of this other young cub, especially considering what happened to the other one. I figured it was just a matter of time. But, to my and the cameramen's surprise, I am sure, the cub was surviving the wild!

I am quite sure that many can pause at this point. Look into your own lives and find the similarities to this story. People who have placed wages on your life and counted you out have been wrong.

Based on who you are, where you come from, to whom you are related, and what others in your family did prior to your arrival. It is a beautiful thing to know that your life is not in their hands. Aren't you glad they cannot write your story because they do not hold the pen? So, Lucky the cub started growing and began to eat smaller rodents to survive in the wild.

There was still a great concern for this young lion because she did not have the skill to hunt because she was separated from her pride prematurely. However, the ability to hunt was lying on the inside but needed to be drawn out. What happen next was amazing! Another female lion was in the wild chasing a baby gazelle and had it cornered. Out of nowhere here comes Lucky to fight off the other female lion. In doing so, it discouraged the other female lion from pursuing the gazelle. Now I am thinking Lucky is getting ready to kill this baby gazelle and eat it, but no! Lucky does the unthinkable and starts protecting it and trying to nurture the gazelle. I am saying to myself this is weird.

So as the program went on, they showed Lucky continuing to protect this gazelle and fighting off countless predators from killing the gazelle. I was astonished at this because I am thinking, "Don't lions eat gazelles?" Why does Lucky keep protecting this gazelle when she should be killing it?

The cameraman was just as amazed as I was watching because he had been studying and watching lions for more than thirty years and had never seen anything like this. He did conclude that if the young lion had not been separated from her pride this would have never happened. What is amazing to me is that two animals, a gazelle and a baby lion, are two lost souls that find one another. The thing they have in common is they both do not know their purpose. Yet they find one another and began a relationship.

The young lion was obviously confused about what her purpose was. Instead of killing this gazelle, the young lion was nurturing and protecting it. So, as I was watching this on television, the Lord Jesus Christ start talking to me about me. He said to me clearly you are a lot like the lion, Lucky.

Things in your life that you should be killing, you are nurturing and protecting them. As you can imagine, I sat there in a bit of a stupor before I figured out what I should do first.

This was a transformational moment in my life. Immediately, when the Lord spoke to me, I felt convicted, as if I needed to move quickly, like run! When it is time to run no one has to tell you. You know it is time to run. Running is usually a quick decision. It is not something you sit up and ponder on all day. Maybe you can relate to what the lord spoke to me concerning my life. Are there things in your life that you have been protecting that you need to kill? Perhaps it is a relationship that you do not want to let go of, family members that you probably need to separate from? Could it be that maybe you are in denial about something that has a stronghold on your life? And it is difficult to let go of it.

Strongholds are not something that are easily detected. Things that hold us back and keep us back are not as obvious as one would think. It is something I like to call a wicked treasure.

I define a wicked treasure as something that you have discovered that it has been hidden and holding you back and just preventing you from going forward. There are many wicked treasures that need to be found.

Lucky the lion was confused about his purpose, he was a lion, but he did not really know it or live it out. Purpose is so essential to success that if you do not know your purpose you could potentially fail. Perhaps you may feel you do not have a purpose and you do not understand why you are here. If you have never heard it before, know and understand that you have a purpose, we all do. Let us use the bumble bee for an example. Bees pollinate a third of everything that we eat. Crops grown for livestock are pollinated by bees. It is not just food crops that rely on bee pollination, cotton does, as well. Annual global crop pollination is estimated to be worth $170 Billion.

I find this to be simply amazing. The whole creation of earth is relying on the bee to be a bee. If the bee tried being anything else, our world would be in trouble.

Who would have ever guessed that the bee had a purpose as such?

I thought bees were like any other pestilent set on earth to annoy me. Did you know there are more than 1.2 million described species of insects in the world? Notice I said described, that just means it is possibly millions of others are undescribed.

Keeping in mind every described and undescribed insect was created with a purpose.

Do not think for one moment I am veering off to something else by talking about the bee. I am still on course of The Run. If you really think about it when you hear the word bee! The first thing that comes to mind is run.

The bee is proof that everything that God makes has a significant purpose. Everything that is created was created with a purpose.

Just think! If the bee did not live in its purpose, it would affect what we eat, how we eat, or if we eat at all.

Our plants would suffer significantly and as a result, so would our livestock that depends on vegetation. Hopefully, this creates a perfect picture of the negative effects that not living in purpose can have.

If we do not live in purpose, we are not living righteously.

Whatever does not live in purpose dies and kills everything it was intended to bring life to. Therefore, run, run, run, on to purpose.

Despair comes to us if we are not living in purpose. Go away with me in your imagination for a few moments.

If the bee has an assignment that is connected to the success of so many necessary things that are vital to our existence, how much more value do you think your life holds? There are things and people that are depending on you to live in your purpose. Then, think on how you can interrupt or abort the potential of their success by not living in purpose.

I can testify of this personally. My dad did not fulfill the purpose of his life and it cut his life short. He died at the young age of forty-five. He left behind unfulfilled promises, gifts, talents, confusion, misunderstandings, abandonment, hurt, and unsolved mysteries.

As a result, I missed out on a lot training and development. I was living my life but, I felt as if I lacked purpose. I thank God daily for interrupting my existence and giving me a sense of purpose.

As a result, I began to run with that purpose. I learned that I am more valuable than many bees. Guess what? So are you! My dad did not fulfill his purpose in life. He seemed to be facing one hard situation after the next. Always seem to have a problem and never a moment of rest. Purpose will always give you rest.

When someone is overwhelmed and tired all the time it could be because they are not living in purpose. A key factor to recognize if you are living in purpose or not is to measure yourself to see what you are accomplishing in life. If you are having the same problems for a long period of time with no resolve it is probably because you are not living in purpose.

Purpose will solve the problem you were not trying to solve. Purpose is equipped with functionality, just like not walking in purpose is equipped with dysfunction. For instance, if I drove my car into the nearby lake, it would destroy my vehicle. The car was not designed to function while being submerged in water.

We are created to solve problems. If problems are attracted to you that you cannot solve, it is a clear indication that you are probably not on the right path.

You are not walking in purpose or maybe it is someone else's purpose to solve it. Because living in purpose solves your problems as well as others you are connected too. I hear it all the time from people when they say they have so many things to do that they are not getting done. I am not talking about on a daily basis. Those individuals you hear say that all the time, I always have so much to do. Purpose helps to simplify our lives. Although you may have days where you may have numerous things to accomplish. Purpose will provoke order in your life. Order means you plan to get things done. Disorder means you will get what you can get done.

There are rules to running. I am not just speaking about the regulations of the rules but what even qualifies you as a participant that could possibly win. Here are a few. 1. What type of physical shape are you in? 2. Have you been training for this? 3. What are you running for? 4. What is your reason for wanting to win? 5. Who are you running against?

These factors have to be determined before you can qualify.

Some of us have never even been in the metaphorical race before because we have not known the answers to these few simple questions. Running without purpose disqualifies you from the race immediately. What race am I talking about? The race that causes you to win in every aspect of life.

There was a time I was working in a convenience store in my young adult life. I would encounter this gentleman running every day at 6am.

He was one of those guys you could set your watch by because he was very consistent. I was thoroughly impressed with this guy, his daily and continuous commitment to running was exceedingly rare to say the least.

I know some would probably say what is so impressive about a guy running every day at 6 am in the morning. At the time I was living in Chicago, Illinois in which the seasons are not always favorable nor conducive for running. This guy was so committed he would run despite the harsh weather.

Allow me to enlighten you on Chicago winters. Six in the morning can be so cold residents will barely want to open the door to get the morning paper. This is not exaggerated by any means.

Most Chicago residents would have just labeled this guy as being completely crazy because no one should even be outside unless they are obligated by employment. However, this guy lived by a different law. Rain, snow or sleet he was out there running daily.

To be successful at running or anything for that matter, you have to establish a daily routine.

What do you do every day? What do you eat every day? Where do you go every day? What do you think every day? And the most important of all! What do you say every day? Is your world being framed by the words you speak? I will answer this last question for you. Yes! Your world is being framed by the words you speak, believe it or not.

If anyone wants to be successful, the first decision is to stop focusing so much on what you are seeing, and start focusing more on what you are saying. *Words are currency that can create a river of opportunities negatively or positively.*

Words are such a powerful instrument. If you master using them effectively you can create wealth, health, love, healing, restoration, relief, and more. Words are valuable according to the worth of the one using the words. For example, if a child tells you that if you keep eating a particular food you will become sick, your health could be threatened. But, if you went to the doctor's office and the doctor tells you the same thing the child told you, who would you believe first?

That all depends on how valuable you think your doctor's words are based on his practice of medicine.

I had to question myself about the things I said daily and to be straightforward, I was not really sure. I have always had a very casual attitude about the things I would say. It is only words, so what harm could they do.

My perspective was sticks and stones could break my bones, but words could never hurt me sort of thing. This is a tremendous lie, not only do words hurt, but they can actually kill you. I think it is quite interesting that if a man is being put to death. His last wishes are not important at all, but they will grant him his last words because they understand that he is getting ready to make a transition. Your last words will uncover what is most important to you. Most people would agree that what was on someone's mind to say before they died is pretty fascinating.

Long ago, a child's first words were pretty important to a mom and dad. But we do not value words the way we use to. Disrespect is at all-time high because of words we hear from children nowadays. The words that are coming from parents to children are equally atrocious. But this is our world.

If we could switch things around and words were money and money was words, it would completely change our world. We would watch the news at night and find out the library had been robbed.

Residents' homes had been broken into and no television, radio, phones, tablets, or any electronic devices were taken but all the manuals were missing. If words were currency! We would be very selective with who we spoke too or if we spoke at all. Banks would no longer have a value. We would be careful with the words we use and how many words we use. Giving someone a piece of your mind in a negative way would not be worth much anymore. Just imagine! Every time someone said that they loved you it would cost them something.

This may surprise a few of you but words are more powerful than money.

For example, remember when Magic Johnson announced that he was HIV positive, and everyone just knew he was going to die.

To everyone's amazement almost forty years later he is still alive and healthy. If you ask most people, they will say that he is alive because he is rich, and he can afford to pay all the money it takes to buy his medicine and keep him healthy. I have had several conversations with people, and this is exactly what they said. He is healthy because he has money, well that is by far one of the dumbest things I have heard.

There were countless wealthy people who died, as a result of having this disease. So, it cannot be just because of money. I think I have the answer! Life and Death lies in the power of the tongue.

While facing a deadly disease that was threatening his life, he decided to speak life into his life. Example, the bible states that while God stepped onto the face of the earth it was dark and void of light, he spoke and said let there be light. The word's that he spoke after announcing he was HIV positive is the reason, I believe he is alive today.

Those words were, "I am going to beat it."

I know this may sound very elementary to some of you but, those of you that know the power of words, do understand what I am saying is true.

We must recondition our minds to not speak what we see but speak what we want to see. Do not be so willing to accept current circumstances even if they are consequences. Circumstances and consequences can be changed with words and actions following. The bible states Proverbs ch.29 v.18 where there is no vision the people perish. If you are going to use your eyes and your eyes tell you there is nothing in front of you, how in the world can you have vision then? You must speak the words to create vision.

When my son was much younger, around the age of three, he would walk up to me and say, "Hey Dad, look I can read."

He would then show me the book he was reading and show me from page to page how well he was reading. As I began to pay closer attention, I discovered he could not read at all.

The book he was reading illustrated the movement of the characters in the book and the words that were written according to the pictures that was on display. My son was able to see the pictures and create the words that he believed that were in front of him. If pictures can create words, then words can create pictures.

Write the vision and make it plain upon tables, that he that run may read it. Habakukuk ch. 2 v.2 kjv.

The best way that I would describe vision in this scenario would be planning. If I could translate the bible, I would revise this statement to say where there is no planning the people perish. I talk to people on a daily basis, young, middle aged, and old.

The common factor that they share is some are excited about the future because they have plans for their future. Others are skeptical about the future because of the present. The current things that are taking place in their lives in their world prevents them from having vision or as I said initially planning. I would go out on the edge with this statement that people who are not planning are walking in darkness. There is no foresight to what is going to happen, so they hold on to things that are going to perish anyway.

Instead of reaching for something that is new they try to give life to something that is going to die anyway. People that are planning are walking in light. This does not mean that they know everything. Although many things will be revealed on their journey. Planning the race helps us to operate in our true nature. Our true nature is to be creative and design according to our plans.

To make something out of nothing is not simply hard work but it is God's work. When we create what was never there, we are living in our true essence. Planning is an indicator that a man can be productive by himself.

Begin planning, cultivate, and saturate your plans. Be assured you will produce if you execute your plans. If we do not produce, it will be because we did not saturate and cultivate the plan. This can provoke a miscarriage of the plans that were to come to life. In a natural birth you cannot predict the day a child will be born without divine intervention, even though I am sure many people have picked the day their child was to be born. When we are planning, we possess the ability to determine the exact birthdate and birthplace of whatever we are planning.

I remember when I recorded my first song. It was unfamiliar ground upon which I was embarking. In my mind, I knew exactly what I wanted the music to sound like.

I sang the song over and over in my head. The day I went to the studio to record the vocals, I was determined to keep the melody that I was hearing in my heart. The musician with whom I was working was able to capture the melody that I wanted, which made me incredibly happy.

This song was my first born so I wanted it to look like me, sound like me, represent everything that would show that this was me and mine alone. I was so nervous because I wanted it to be good. The length of the song was about 3 minutes and 28 seconds long. There were many concerns I had because I did not want the music to be better than my singing nor did I want my singing to be better than the music. I was hoping for a perfect marriage where the vocals and the music became one. Hearing my vocals recorded made me cringe because I hated the way I sounded on the track. It was not to my liking. The musician was encouraging because she reassured me that I sounded great and to just relax. So, I accepted the advice I was being given and just said okay.

When I first heard the song, I was filled with so much joy because I loved it.

I was amazed it was me that had written and arranged the song. This song was good. It is like a newborn child being born. You know it is real once you hear the baby crying. That is exactly how I felt when I heard my song for the first time. When I looked back on me making that first song, I really did not have any plans for the song and what I wanted to do with it.

The focus was just making the song. There were not any plans or ideas that I had for it. It would have been nice to sell it and generate an income. To do something with it by getting it into the right person's hands.

The song was extremely near and dear to me because it was my first. This song was the first experience I had of a description of The Run. Remember I said *The Run* is the starting point, the discovery moment. *The Run* is the get the ball rolling and get out of the space and place of unfamiliarity. The Run is to just get it going. This was the moment when inspiration just hit me, and I did not know what I was going to do. But I knew that it was something I could be doing. The song is still sitting abandoned. This song applies to that very scripture. Proverbs ch.29 18 without a vision the people perish.

Now do not get me wrong, I do not have any regrets about not planning for the song, but If I could do it all over again, there would have been a plan created first. Then afterward, I probably would have recorded more songs and sold them. Guess what? The day is not over. There will be more recorded songs from me that I plan to write, sing, arrange, and possibly even produce.

The experience showed me that faith is moving without the answers. Notice I did not say faith is moving without vision. Faith creates vision and answers are found in the way of the journey. Fear will try to create false vision. False vison tells you that you must have answers before you can move. Most of the time you will hear people say that they need to know everything before they can make one move. That is not realistic in the way that life unfolds.

Vision comes first and provision follows. Thereafter, plans and dreams can be achieved. Plan your life like Jesus Christ is never coming back. But live your life like he is coming back tomorrow. The statement sounds contrary to one another. Living is what we all currently are doing. Planning is what we get to accomplish if we live.

I discovered for me that running was a great way to relieve stress along with unloading the daily weights of everyday life. It also gave me the opportunity to get alone with my own thoughts.

Running showed me how to become a winner all the time, I would set a goal to run daily and because of my follow through I was always able to win. Running created the opportunity for me to talk to God and I was not even trying to. One day, I was on my way to run and I remember that I was thinking about some money I had coming in.

As I began to think on this money, I was so excited about it, the first thing that came to my mind was to make sure I tithe with this money that was coming in. My mother instilled in me early on that ten percent of my income was God's money and you do not touch it. By the way, anyone that does not know what tithe means it just means that you owe God ten percent of your income. So, I continued running with this thought in mind. I have got to tithe with this money because I have never had to tithe off this much income. At that moment, I was feeling really good about myself because I knew it was a lot of money and I wanted God to be proud of me.

In my mind, I am just running and running happily and all I am thinking about is tithe, tithe, tithe I cannot wait to tithe. Then I heard the voice of the Lord speak to me and He said, I want you to tithe with your life. It showed me right then and there that God is not impressed with money. I was so blessed by this because it showed me God did not want my money, he wanted me.

Now do not take this the wrong way and think that now you do not have to tithe to your church and give money. That is not what I am saying, and you know it!

Money is one of the most important things to God. Not because he needs money, but he understands how important it is to us. Money affords us almost anything that we want and need. So, when you take it and give it to the God. We are showing him how much we trust and love him. That is an example of worship to God.

Taking the very thing that can give food, shelter, and clothing, not to mention countless other things. We serve a very jealous God. Anything that takes precedence over him is offensive. But the point of my story is to show how much God loves us. The scripture clearly says that where your treasure is so will your heart be.

Whatever you give your money to or invest your money in continuously, you begin to pay remarkably close attention to your investment.

Does your heart follow your money? Or does your money follow your heart. Instruct your heart to follow something and watch and see how well it does. Then give your money away continuously or invest your money and watch your heart follow that money without you giving it instruction or permission. If someone is not sure about where their heart is tied to, there is a simple solution to finding the answer. I will give you a hint, it starts with a money trail. Track wherever your money is going then your heart is linked directly. Jesus proved this principle in Matt: Ch;19 v.16-22 with the young rich ruler.

The young rich ruler was bragging about his ability and commitment to keep the law and the commandments of God. He stated that he kept the law from the time he was a kid unto that present time. Jesus turned to him and gave him a new commandment. Go sell all you have and follow me, and you will then have treasure in heaven. Then, the story states that the young rich ruler walked away incredibly sad. Jesus' words made him sad but why?

Jesus knew that his heart was not right with God. Perhaps the young rich ruler walked away sad because he just then discovered that his heart was tied more to his possessions than it was tied to God. He was not willing to lose his possessions, but he was willing to sacrifice his relationship with God over worldly possessions. Anyone that chooses anything over God will not remain happy. Choosing anything over God will put us in a world of sadness. The story never gave the young rich ruler's name. The story just said he was rich. If you pay close attention to the story, it told us how he became rich.

The young rich ruler stated he had kept the laws and commandments of God from his youth up unto the present moment in his life. He was rich because he kept the law of God. No one can keep the laws and the commandments of God and remain poor. The young rich ruler had thought he had been running a marathon. By keeping the laws and the commandments for such a long time. I would say that he did run a marathon, but the course changed when the time came for him to run a sprint and sell all that he had and follow Jesus.

The young rich ruler failed miserably. The marathon takes a long time to accomplish. He had invested all of his time into the marathon for years. Then, at a moment's notice, he was being commanded to go and sell all that he accomplished in a moment's time. It had to be difficult to part with what he had. The young rich ruler had loss his focus. He forgot that how he became rich was keeping the commandments and the laws of God. The very same thing can happen to anyone that places more value on what that have and forgetting the way they got it in the first place.

Just recently I was doing my daily jog and everything in me was hurting. My muscles were tightening, legs start cramping, and I just felt sort of bloated and winded at the same time. All of these, discoveries were a sure indicator that I should stop and go home. That is when I turned on a new mindset, I told myself you are not going to stop and give up.

Keep going until your legs stop cramping, muscles stop tightening and everything stops hurting. Shifting my thoughts really worked for me in a great way.

The pain did not stop, nor did my muscles stop tightening, and neither did my legs stop cramping. However, I just decided to ignore what I was feeling and push my way through.

I have news for you friends, a lot of negative occurrences and distractions will surface in your life at very inopportune times, but just push through and keep going.

In a race, everyone wants the gold medal. Not the silver, or the bronze, but the gold. The gold is the most coveted piece of medal. Maybe because it is the most valuable, or could it be because of what it is made of? The gold is always the objective. If the goal is to get the gold, it is a question of will. A will is something you do not normally hear much about. It is not an everyday normal conversation. I think the reason being has to do with the fact that it is synonymous with death.

There are very few people who enjoy having conversations surrounding death. It can become very unsettling for some people.

The majority time, we do not hear people talking about wills unless someone has recently died and left a fortune behind to be divided.

A will should not be just written for the end of your life but throughout one's life of accomplishments. I am certain that if you are reading this book, you could write a will right now, not a traditional will in the sense of what you will leave behind when you die.

But, in the sense of what you will leave right now to accomplish your goals and dreams. It is things and people in your life right now that you should part with. Letting go of the old and embracing the new is not as easy of a task as it sounds. It can really be quite challenging.

We write wills every day, anytime we say that we will or will not do something. The only thing that we lack is documents to write it on. Contrary to popular belief, every word we speak is being recorded. I know what you are thinking, cells phones, electronic devices, the government, powers that be, are recording us.

While that might be true, that is not what I am talking about at all. I will challenge you write now stop reading this book and start writing a will for yourself right now. Let it start something like this....

I *will* stay in control of my emotions. I *will* mine my own business today. I *will* only speak positive words about myself and others. I *will* pay attention to how much effect my attitude contributes to the atmosphere.

I wrote a will when I was 19yrs old, I confessed my sins and asked the Lord to save my soul and He did. I have this assurance that when I die my soul WILL not be left behind, but I WILLED it to my Savior. My question is not who gets your antique cars, houses, land, clothes, shoes, and your personal belongings. Who gets your soul? Decide to whom you are going to *will* your soul.

It is the only thing we have that will never die. Most of us are conditioned to pursuit success as possibility rather than an actuality. Therefore, success becomes more of a thing of luck and being in the right place at the right time. As opposed to setting goals that are aligned with your God given purpose.

The overall idea is to have a successful life. But so many of us will not achieve a successful life because we do not even know how to have a successful day. We do not know what the *run* of life is all about. If you do not know how to make a good donut, you do not need to make a dozen. You must ask yourself, what does a successful day look like? Stop! Take a few moments and think about this. What does a successful day look like?

The first thing that must be done is to determine what am I trying to accomplish and why? What am I aiming for and what is my targeted goal for the day? Success cannot be predicated on the actions of anyone else but your own. When failure happens in life it is usually linked to someone judging the actions of everyone else but their own.

If you are not where you want to be because of the actions of someone else, then you are a failure. If you are where you want to be because of your own actions, then you are a success. Success requires personal accountability, while failure requires personal dependence on other's abilities.

The confidence should always be on oneself because of your ability. When you place a demand on others ability, it is not confidence, it has now become a wager. That is why so many people fail at gambling. Gambling is putting confidence into something or someone else to win for you. This is a huge mistake.

I remember hearing stories of Michael Jordan being a big gambler. I do not know him personally, but what I understood about his gambling is he was placing bets on his abilities to golf. It is not gambling when you are betting on your abilities. It is gambling when you are betting on your inabilities.

Running appeals to me because it has a built-in success ratio in the sense that I am placing my confidence in my abilities alone. At times it is tempting to shift the responsibility of someone else to win for you. Do not get me wrong here, I am not saying that we do not need help and assistance at some point. But do not shift the responsibility of success from yourself to others. The biblical story comes to mind as it relates to this thought about Adam and Eve. In the Garden of Eden, Adam's responsibility was to dress, keep the garden, and keep the commandment of the Lord to not eat of the tree of knowledge of good and evil. As the story goes, Eve offered Adam the fruit and he did eat it.

When confronted by the Lord about his responsibility, he shifted the responsibility and blamed to Eve for his failure.

I cannot emphasize this enough. If you are not where you want to be because of the actions of others, you are a failure. But if you are where you want to be because of your own actions, then you are a success.

When running on my daily run I would have my ear buds in listening to something inspirational that would keep me motivated. The first mile that I would run there would be a notification that was audible that would say one mile and tell me how much time it took to run that first mile. This was a very key point to me because it was an indication if I had an opportunity to improve my previous time.

If that notification told me that my time was the same, a bit more, or less, I would keep the same pace that I was going.

But if I got that notification that I was much earlier than my previous time. The competitive juices would begin to rise in me. Although this was not a part of my goal, it challenged me to reach my goal at a much faster pace than I intended.

You can discover goals inside of your goals. That first mile would set the pace for my entire run on my days out. That first mile would dictate what type of run I would have.

Through my experiences I have come to realize that when something comes first, or it is placed first, it sets the initial desire and every desire after is attached until ignored or satisfied.

For example, if you wake up in the morning and the first thing you eat is a cheeseburger with fries and a soda, that meal is probably going to set the course of your appetite for the entire day. Do not get me wrong. I am not saying that you will not have a mindset or a desire for anything healthy but, you will crave the same type of junk food you started with that day. If you start your day off with a healthy nutritious breakfast and when your done you feel great, you immediately know you ate the right foods because your body feels nourished, you are not weighed down by what you just ate. This is what you know for certain based on how your body is responding.

The next moment you decide to eat, your body will be craving another nutritious meal. But our minds our framed by our habits.

When we tend to eat the wrong foods, in our mind it will cause a war against the mind and your body. So, we must eat the right foods for a long period of time until our minds shift to the habit of eating correct foods. Once the mind and the body are in harmony with one another. Not only will task become so much easier, but life will also be much easier and enjoyable.

Most athletes understand you must train your body, in order to get the correct physical functionality out of it. Let me tell you, there must be a continual and perpetual training for the mind as well as the body.

The emphasis is always placed on the body. Maybe you are working on your legs, calf muscles, or thighs. Maybe you are working your arms, shoulders, biceps, and triceps. Let us not forget about the show piece, center piece which is the chest and stomach.

The chest and the stomach are like the living and dining room of the house. Just long as these two rooms are in order, the house looks clean.

We must not allow the body to train the mind. The mind must train the body. The word train is very necessary here because the trainer must be the leader. The trainee is the follower. Again, the mind must be the trainer and the body must be the trainee. If the body trains the mind, then the mind is being disabled and being prevented from thinking. When the mind feeds the body then the body can develop properly.

The body is developed through inspiration. Such as nose=smell, mouth=taste, ears=sound, hands=feel and eyes=sight.

These are the avenues that develops the body. Through these vehicles the body loses or gains strength by having them fed or not fed. Animals are trained by their bodies.

They are very well developed by their environment. They are well practiced in their habitat. Sound, smell, taste, feel and sight is how the body eats. Animal intellect is based upon theirs bodies. Animal senses are ten times heightened than human beings.

If they could earn a PHD, I believe they would have it in sound, smell, taste, feel, and sight. The mind has the power to overtake these bodily advantages that the animal possesses.

That is why man has been known to capture animals. Although, quite a few animals have been known to capture man. But the point I am making is the mind possesses the ability to trump everything. The mind eats much differently than the body.

What causes the mind to grow is information not inspiration. This is how the mind grows and develops. Information is the food and nutrient of the mind. Do we feed our minds as much as we feed our bodies?

Most of us can answer this question without thinking about it too much.

I am willing to bet that majority of us feed the body more than the mind. The mind and the body should be fed at the same level and capacity on a continual basis. If not, there is going to be a continual imbalance. The mind and the body will be out of sync and function without harmony.

Have you ever watched someone dance fast to a slow song?

No matter how beautiful the song, or how well the individual is dancing. If there is no harmony the ear cannot enjoy the music and the eyes cannot enjoy the dancing. Although, they may work very well individually.

It is nothing more than tragedy on display. What if someone described our lives as such.

It may seem like a cruel observation but, it may be an appropriate assessment based upon the lack of harmony that is being exhibited in one's life. Harmony is usually described as two or more individuals or instruments working simultaneously. All it takes is for one to be working out of sync to forfeit the sound that is to be accomplished.

Going back to speaking about the mind. Think about the many thoughts we have in our minds daily.

Are your thoughts running in harmony with one another? Or are you a scattered brain thinker that allows your emotions to make selections for you.

If your thoughts do not align properly, it will become exceedingly difficult to accomplish a task. It will come to a point where it becomes difficult to accomplish anything. I can personally relate to this because it was me at one point and time. Numerous thoughts would go through my mind of what I wanted to accomplish just on daily basis.

Seldomly, would I put things in sequence. As a result, I struggled with accomplishing tasks. Things run much more smoothly when they are put in alignment. We all have so much in our heads and extraordinarily little is written down. We put too much pressure on the memory bank when we leave it all on the inside. There must be continual withdraws from the mind that are transformed into visual aids.

I know it is considered old school to write it down. But whatever avenue you decide to select, make sure it will give you a way to look at it and make necessary adjustments.

One day I was in my bedroom and news was on the television. The news was reporting a story about bear attacks. The news anchor reported that a particular park people had suffered bear attacks.

My mind went into a frenzy immediately because I have a friend that is an avid hiker. The park that he would hike in is the same park and I was concerned for his safety.

The next day, I knew I would get a chance to see him. When I saw him, he was at a great distance from me. So, I yelled out to him. As he walked up to me and said, "What's up?" I told him about what I had learned about bear attacks in the park that he would frequently hike in.

Brian looked and me and laughed. He said, "Why are you so worried? I know exactly what to do if a bear tries to attack."

The look on my face told the entire story. In my mind I was saying he is crazy and will probably get mauled by a bear. There I was in a state of amazement because he did not share the same concern. I am a city boy. I am used to fast cars, traffic, loud noises, 24hour stores, and restaurants. A city that sleeps, but not that much.

On the other hand, my friend Brian grew up in the country and was more familiar with wildlife animals.

As I was continuing to have these thoughts about how naïve he was, Brian began to explain to me, how bears behave. What their likes and dislikes were. How they viewed circumstances, what attracts them, and what discourages them. After a short conversation with Brian and his knowledge of bears, it changed my fear for him. I started to be more concerned for bears and what would happen to them if they ran into Brian. Bears are similar to most animals in the sense that they depend heavily on their sense of smell. The nose and mouth are the deciding agents for what is good and bad. What happens in our natural world is the same thing that is happening in our spiritual world. The common symptoms to Covid-19 are loss of smell and taste. If you cannot smell and you cannot taste, then you do not have the ability to judge what is right and what is wrong to eat.

Some have lost their ability to discern what is right and what is wrong. Some are calling wicked people righteous and righteous people wicked. We are fighting against justice and promoting injustice. If you cannot smell or taste you are not the hunter anymore. You are now the hunted.

If we cannot smell and taste metaphorically, we are going to be more susceptible to strong deception and delusion.

We can be placed under the control of the enemy because we cannot smell, and we cannot taste. We must depend on someone else to tell us what is good and what is evil. They have made us believe the only way you could die is Covid-19. So therefore, they will make a vaccination a requirement. It does not matter if you are not sick or have ever contracted the disease.

There will be a requirement to take it. Can you smell and taste that something is not, right? Would you take chemotherapy if you never had cancer? If you can smell and taste, then you cannot be controlled.

Now the question rises on the inside of me to ask. How much knowledge do you have of your enemy or potential enemy that you could be facing? The enemy is a master strategist. He studies and waits patiently to ensure his success ratio. The moment you cannot pick up on his scent is the moment he is gaining ground on you to attack you at your most vulnerable moment. You need smell and taste to run the race.

One day I was walking through my neighborhood just getting some exercise and I remember just being in my own head and really focusing on the things I was thinking about. As I was walking, I felt like something was with me or was watching me. So, I paused and looked to my left and there was a domestic cat sitting right on top of a wooden fence with his eyes locked right on me.

Who can say? How long had that cat been sitting there? Was it stalking me from afar?

What is startling is that I was not able to see of feel the presences of the cat until I was in the danger zone. Very much off balance and unprepared for an attack with no clue of how to counter. Although I know this cat was not going to attack me, it made me think of other predators.

Hunting is when the prey is caught off guard and does not have any clue that it is being pursued. The enemy loves to attack our ignorance and our arrogance. These two characteristics have been bound together throughout human history.

Arrogance and ignorance are dangerous individually, but when coupled together we can become more susceptible to erroneous behavior if we possess them. Arrogance and ignorance are revealed knowledge. More commonly than not these can be obviously on display, which is more subjective in its natural manifestation. This is just my opinion through my own experiences. While most of the time arrogance and ignorance is visibly revealed, I believe it holds more truth when it is invisible but discovered.

This is what I would describe as a wicked treasure. For example, you can see a person dressed in fancy clothes that sets them apart from everyone else. They may have a way about them that shows they are not to be approached. Also, they may have an expression on their face as if they are annoyed by the atmosphere, they must share with people who are undeserving of their presence. Their facial frown gives hint that they may be accustomed to the finer things in life, but abhors anything or anyone that does not meet a presumed status. This can also be very misleading because it is what shows on the surface.

By the same token, you can have a person wearing quite common looking clothes that are neutral colors, but they display a consistent smile.

They are pleasant, approachable, complimentary, and seem to have a magnetic attraction about them.

However, they have a noticeably quiet way about them. They do not show a confidence about their esteem or an idea of an elevated lifestyle. Remember this is what is displayed on the surface. Now if there was a wager to be placed based on the characteristics that was describe, the description of the first person would be selected as ignorance and arrogance.

The description of the second would probably be humility and wisdom. Both answers may have been acceptable for yesteryear, but we now reside in a much more sophisticated and complex society that what looks actual is what is visual. *But what is truly actual is what is invisible.* We have been trained to think that what we see is what is real. Is it a wonder why clothing stores use mannequins to get their ideas across? They can dress a mannequin and position them in the store in a stance and people automatically think they know exactly what any person is all about based on that attire.

Both characteristics are pathways to destruction, just as wisdom and humility are pathways to success. Take these thoughts and concepts and put them into action. Then go and achieve exactly what you desire. Do not take your time about it. Get in a hurry and run on to success. It has been waiting for you at the finish line for a while. Success is always waiting on us while failure is hoping that we sit back and wait for others. In a race, it is a starting line, and it is a finish line. Failure is starting the race and never finishing. Success is starting the race and finishing.

CHAPTER 2

The Sprint
Extraordinary People Sprint in Necessary Times

It is what separates average from extraordinary, normal from abnormal, excellence from perfection, Clark Kent from Superman, and 1st place from 2nd place. This is the place where you fit in or you do not. In this particular space you must know that you belong there. It is where the best line up and only the elite gathers. The competition is very stiff because there can be only one winner.

There is little room for error if any at all. Your focus must be sharp, pointed, and precise. The sprint could be compared to open heart surgery because one wrong move could put success in jeopardy. There have been great sprinters in the last three decades. Just on memory alone, I can think of at least ten of the greatest sprinters that have ever existed.

The faces have changed and the styles of running vastly different from one another. However, the fact remains they were all amazingly fast at one point or another. The most enticing thing about the sprint is that it is an exceedingly small window of time you must give your best or it will be buried and never discovered. I am certain that you are familiar with the term, *use it or lose it*! Yes! That is what the sprint is all about.

In the sprint there is no time to pace yourself or strategize, it all happens so quickly in that moment of time. There is no time for 1st gear, 2nd gear, or 3rd gear. You do not get that luxury in the sprint. You have got to give it everything you have and leave it right where you left it.

This is arguably the most difficult race that there is because competition is always at your heels or on them. You have to decide very quickly if you would win or lose. In any race losing can be a humbling experience. But, in the sprint winning can also be a humbling experience depending on how one views their victory. When the winner realizes that they have won -- but they barely won.

It can begin to chip away at your confidence and cause you to second guess yourself. The sprinter begins to think I could have lost, and if they are not careful, they will begin to prepare themselves for defeat.

Never second guess yourself if you plan on being first.

As a small child among my friends and family, there was little that concerned me as for most children. Nevertheless, being fast was a top priority no matter what the situation or circumstance were. Being first was something that is ingrained in most children early in developing stages, whether we are aware or unaware.

In my home life, being first to ask for something, being first to tell your side of the story, being first to have something that no one else had, being first to do something unique or creative, was always to command a positive response. The spoils of being first always equated to reward, approval, validation, acceptance, or just some means of self-worth and confidence. When I think on these things now, it amazes me how so many of these things still have not changed much. We are all still looking for some of the same things we first initially desired.

Over the years of my experience and observation, I have learned that your purpose must far exceed your ability because that will in turn cause your ability to reach maximum potential. I remember a time being in grade school and my mom had just purchased a brand-new coat for me. It was a coat I had been wanting for a while and I had finally received it. I was overwhelmed with happiness.

I prepared for school and got myself ready and went to grab my new coat only to hear my mother say, "Do not play football in that coat!"

My classmates and I played football in the morning before school, and football was my only motivation for being on time for school. The type of football that we played was quite rough, kid's pants would get ripped, hoods torn off from their coat, a lot of kids could get hurt and they did.

However, it was the risk we were all willing to take. So, there I was on my way to school and when I arrived as usual there were my classmates inviting me to come and join in and play. I could not resist my desire to go and play against my mother's instructions not to. I was not as disobedient as you may assume but I knew my mother's concern was me tearing up a brand-new coat.

Therefore, I determined I could make it so that we both would get what we wanted which meant I had to make sure that I could play without tearing it up. This was a very risky move on my part because kids were trying to tackle to get a hold of you by any means necessary. My coat had a hood on it which made it easier for someone to catch me from behind. Any type of loose clothing can be detrimental when you are trying to prevent someone from catching you.

This meant I had to be incredibly fast, but what happen next will shock you, but it did not shock me. I played football for about 45 minutes and out of group of about twenty kids my age not one person was able to not just tackle me but to touch me. I was fully persuaded that if my mom found out I was playing in that coat I would be in serious trouble.

So, I was not playing just for fun. My purpose was to not tear up my coat. After we all finished playing football that morning all the kids were saying to me, "Man, you were so fast today. What in the world got into you?"

Little did they know it was not what got into me, it was about who could tear into me. They would say, I knew you were fast but, I did not know you were that fast.

Let us look a bit deeper into the statement that I previously mentioned about my coat that had with the hood attached. That hood on the coat made it easier for my opponents to be able to catch, stop and prevent me from accomplishing my goals which at the time was getting to the goal.

The loose clothing and untied shoes, tassels, or belt hanging off your person can give your opponent an advantage to attack and stop you from reaching your accomplishments. I am sure you have noticed that if you ever watched a football game the men are wearing tight pants, everything on them fits rather closely to prevent from easier contact.

When you are trying to run, loose clothing can take away your effectiveness and efficiency. Running on a daily basis uncovered this very truth.

One day on my run, I was wearing basketball shorts which are very baggy shorts that swing frontward and backward. Also, the shirt I was wearing was about two sizes too big. It was a day I wanted to be comfortable running, but little did I know these loose clothes would be contrary to my intent.

During the beginning of my run the wind began to pick up and it began to affect my run. The loose clothing caught the wind and slowed me down and decreased my momentum. This was happening with my shorts and my shirt. Eventually the wind began to calm, and I was able to get right back into a rhythm.

While I was running for such a long period of time I began to sweat profusely. This is quite normal when I go on my runs, but this time my loose clothing absorbed all the sweat. It made me heavier and caused my run to be more of a challenge. If I were wearing the properly fitted clothing when the wind hit me, it would have hit me and kept going and not create a delay.

Also, while I was sweating the sweat that was making my attire heavier would have just rolled off my body. I could have released the wind and the sweat instead of storing it on my person. These minor issues had an enormous effect on my ability to produce the results I anticipated. We all must be careful of the wind and loose clothing in life. I know you are saying, "What is the wind and loose clothing in life?"

It could be friends, family, associates, coworkers, and people that have access to your life. People that slow you down and weigh you down. People that do not add to your life, but they subtract from your life.

While some people desire more friends and relationships, some of us need to get friends, family members, associates that fit into our lives to help us accomplish our purpose. Stop allowing people to hang around and hang on to your life that are not adding to it and prompting you to greatness. Apply this story to your personal life.

Do not attract the predators that will look for the same advantage to annihilate you. Are there things in your life that are hanging off you? Just like the pair of untied shoes, are there things in your life that you left untied, unsettled, or idle? Let me be the first one to tell you, they will not just go away. Relationships are a great example of unresolved matters and issues that when people are done with dealing with one another they just walk away. Walking away does not resolve matters it just prolongs them from being addressed. Getting back to my football story.

This was the first time in my life that I understood that running with a purpose would increase my abilities and push me to levels I never experienced before.

It was not just about my athletic ability as much as it was about what was driving me on the inside.

There is a saying that is in the sports world that goes like this. "*You can't teach speed.*" Every team and coach know that if you have the weapon of speed in your arsenal then you are much more dangerous than your competitors. Speed can be the difference between winning and losing, quick commercial break, as my mentor would say.

This is a pivot to let you know I am about to go off subject, but not topic. In the wild many predators would love to eat a gazelle but there are only a select few that are fast enough to catch one. You may have guessed -- it is the cheetah! It possesses the ability to catch any prey they want.

What a wonder gift to possess. While most predators are subjected to eat whatever they can because of their limited skills.

Cheetahs can eat whatever they want because of what they are naturally born to do. If there was human emotion in the animal kingdom, I am sure many animals would be jealous of the cheetah. Not because the cheetah is better, greater, or has more significance.

We as humans tend to compare who we are to what we are not. Whatever you keep your eyes upon is what you will value. Value can change quite often based upon a variety of things.

For example, seasons change value immediately. I cannot just go outside dressed in beach clothes in the winter seasons. The clothes have no value in cold climates. Some people are fortunate enough to live in places where there is just one season. Do not get me wrong here, when I am talking about seasons, I'm not just talking about weather. There will be times when everything is going well and then everything is a challenge. You can have a business that is pretty much running by itself because it is doing so well.

Then there can be times where you are just having a hard time paying the bills. When seasons change, it does not just expose the fragileness of nature and its elements. It also exposes the character and the integrity of us human beings. Anyone can be positive, chipper, and grateful when things are going well. But who can display these same characteristics when things are not?

Being the same all the time takes continual practice of good and bad occurrences and you as an individual maintaining your same posture. I hold a great deal of respect for people that show gratitude. Gratitude is an attribute that I admire most because it is something that must be developed over time. You just cannot go to the store and buy it or receive it as a gift or inheritance. It happens when an individual looks at their life's circumstances and makes the assessment that things will not always be good, nor will things always be bad. Things being good and bad are just a natural part of a life's cycle. We all want great things for our kids and want to prevent them from having experiences that will frustrate, stall, and interrupt their progress in life.

So many of our youth are being raised and developed in artificial environments that only serve as delays for consequences that they will eventually meet.

The sprint is the smallest race in comparison to the relay, the marathon long distance events. The sprint 100m race has the least number of participants with the shortest distance to run. The responsibility of winning and losing is all placed on one individual. When it comes to the sprint it is noticeably short lived, it is not a throne that you can sit on and enjoy very long. The sprint is similar to the dance. When you show up to the dance you have got to be ready to dance. Just like the sprint you cannot slip, hesitate, stumble, or second guess your ability. The average 100m race is over in about twelve seconds. Can you just imagine you have twelve seconds to give your absolute best? All the hours, days, weeks, and months of training and preparing are about to be judged in about twelve seconds. This is just a little insight to see how difficult this race can be.

Who would like to put that type of pressure on themselves? I personally do not even think it is fair considering all the dedication and time one would put in it and then be judged in twelve seconds. The sprint obviously takes a lot of courage and self-confidence to even want to be in the race.

Do not misunderstand, I do not want to make it sound hopeless, but it will require perfection. It makes sense why it commands so much adoration and praise when there is a winner. A race is only considered a big event when the competition is well matched. The type of competition that is so evenly matched that it requires a race because a winner cannot be chosen, it must be decided. As I just said previously in the previous chapter, all the pressure is on the person to win or lose the race. Knowing your event and being sure of what is lying on the inside of you is a true starting point. The sprint is not a team sport. Those of you that are old enough to remember the NBA great Michael Jordan.

He was very sure of his sport and his basketball capabilities, but he was not sure of his event. Michael Jordan tried to run a sprint in a relay race.

Starting in 1989 and thereafter, he took his team to the playoffs that would lose to the Detroit Pistons in spectacular fashion. Keep in mind the Detroit Pistons had individual players that had the ability to dominate any player. The difference between the Detroit Pistons team and Michael Jordan was the Pistons knew their event. They understood they were not running a sprint but running a relay race. In a relay race there are quite a few teams all made up of four individuals. The event requires each member to pass the baton to activate the next members ability to dominate.

The baton is passed three different times to four individuals. Michael Jordan would keep the baton the entire race and lose the game. All because he was not willing to ignite his teammates to explode and dominate. Michael could easily dominate each man individually, and he did, but he could not dominate them collectively.

After many failed attempts he decided to depend on someone else. So, he changed his event to the relay race and stop running sprints. Once he understood his event, he raised the level of his individual dominance while igniting the dominance of his teammates, as well.

The rest is history, he brought the city of Chicago six championship titles. If things in your life are not adding up and you keep coming against obstacles that you cannot overcome, maybe you need to ask yourself if you are in the right race. Or maybe you are in the right race just the wrong event. The sprint is lived in a short moment in time and then fades away. Dance is remarkably similar to the sprint because it has a short-term contract, as well.

Even though you may witness many older and elderly people dancing and competing, it is understood it is a young person's event. Dance is a supremely energetic event that usually requires youth and raw talent that can be developed quickly and launched. The dance world is usually a reflection of very toned and shapely figures that have spent a great deal of time mastering their craft.

Dance sometime requires fast, strong, precise, agile, and graceful movements. In dance there are quite a few risky moves that are involved. A dancer must be willing to compromise their body to flex, turn, twist, jump, fall, and to be courageous in ways that the average person is not willing to attempt. This is a mindset that applies to other areas in our life. It is important to take on this same level of flexibility just like the dancer. When we are facing new circumstances that we have never seen before. We must make the required adjustments to get the correct outcome. Keeping the same posture in certain scenarios will prevent innovation which will discourage motivation. Runners who would participate in the hurdles race could not keep the same posture as other runners in any other event. In the hurdles race there is consistent jumping, landing, and keeping your balance. The race is run with a particular rhythm and gracefulness. It reminds me of a deer in the forest running and jumping without any care in the world. When a deer sees open space, they are in their element and cannot be stopped unless they are challenged by a faster predator.

A deer needs to see open space, or it will become dumbfounded and disturbed. This is symbolic to the term, a deer caught in head lights. Deer do not think, they just react and usually react very quickly, that is why they suffer many mishaps. They possess the ability to outrun most of their opponents but, do not possess the ability to outthink them. The hunters of the big cats are not the male lions. The male lions are to protect the territory and kill anything that threatens that territory. The female lion is the hunter, the one that studies it prey's behavior, routines, and movements. As a result of their skill, they are able to catch deer and other prey.

I remember a time speaking with a gentleman, and we were talking about deer and he said I do not understand why God made deer so dumb. He was referring to an incident where he lived in a town and would encounter deer on a daily basis. The deer would stand in the streets and would not move. This frustrated him in such a way that he wanted to move elsewhere or have the deer removed from the town.

The deer had been taken out of their natural habitat. Therefore, they exhibited abnormal behavior. This is not just a commonality with animals but with us as people. When they are not in their element or necessary environment, they will struggle to produce greatness, brilliance, and uniqueness, that thing that separates you from everyone else. We must be willing to take the risk on of trying something new. Although we still need to know what environment we need to be in to not just survive but produce the best of our abilities.

In the sprint there is an understanding that someone else is always coming for that seat. This event is not the later on let me get prepared event, it is the right now event.

The Sprint raises this question, can you win with everything that is you in this moment? For the sprint, you must always be prepared at any given moment. If things in your life began to fall apart at this very minute, how fast could put it back together again? If you lost your job, family, skills, connections, or an important source of income, how quickly could you recover?

There is no time to think and gather thoughts in the sprint, you must react. The sprint uncovers what is lying on the inside of us.

I think that ninety nine percent of the time we measure ourselves and others by what we can see with the visible eye. But I do not think we look at things enough with the eye of understanding. For example, when we look at a car, we look at the color, size, shape, amenities, accommodation, benefits, and how much of a reflection it is of who we are.

Then at times we have the tendency to look at people based on these same characteristics. Too often, we look at the car and never check to see what type of engine the car has, or what was the purpose for this car when it was being made? When, I was a single man, I had an extremely fast car that I adored. The car was an SS Monte Carlo two door, the color was bright red with tinted windows, automatic start, and a great sound system just to name a few things. But that car and I had a short time together because I got married about a year later. When I bought that car, I loved the color and how fast it was. I knew it would be the perfect car for me.

Being married with kids changed my purpose. It did not matter that I wanted the car, it was not beneficial to have when it was not built for a family. The car was made for a single person not for someone with a large family that it could not accommodate. Marriage changed my purpose, so the things and tools I was equipped with while single had to be replaced. When your purpose change it changes the tools that you use.

One day my son and I were going for a walk and I asked him a question, something that I do quite often with him.

I said, "Son do you know what the word abuse means"? He gave me, what I would call the best answer ever.

He said yes, "It's when you don't use something the right way."

His answer was so profound because whatever you use the wrong way is going to either be destroyed or it will self-destruct and will come to its end.

Living in Chicago practically my whole life the winters could get very brutal. When going outside in those winter months, you must protect your good shoes. The best way to protect them is to not wear them at all. Any shoes that are not made to endure snow and salt are going to be destroyed. I had experiences with this on a few occasions. There was a pair of all white leather tennis shoes that I had and really liked, and I thought looked great with the clothes I was wearing that day. So, I went out in the snow in those shoes. My feet were a little cold, but I made it through the rough snowy day.

When I arrived home later that day and took off my shoes, I set them in the corner and just went about my business. A few days passed and wanted to wear the shoes again. As I looked at my shoes, I noticed that the paint was faded on different parts of the shoe. I had made it through that snowy day, but my tennis shoes had not.

The shoe looked as if it had aged, it was completely ruined, and there was nothing I could do about it.

The lesson that I learned that day was these shoes look nice, but they are not made for the snow. What is the purpose for which something is created? The kitchen is created to prepare, store, cook, and eat food. It is the place where the allure of different aromas will attract you to that area.

What is cooked in the kitchen usually can be smelled throughout the entire house. The kitchen is an open space that usually does not have a door. The bathroom with a door serves another purpose.

The improper use of something will always create problems, just as the proper use of something creates resolutions. Here comes a fork in the road.

Giving people what they want just because they are complaining is the greatest example of weak leadership. Passing laws that help to accommodate individual's deficits will only swell to more misfortune. Many leaders in our world are not showing that they are visionaries at all. They are just leaders who have sight but no vision. The ability to see what is only in front of them as they make decisions and pass laws in favor of groups of people who will help to ensure another term so they can keep their seat in office. They never take into consideration the laws that they are passing will eventually be a part of the ingredients that will destroy this nation.

The Jesus principle fits perfectly in this scenario. The principle of leaving the ninety-nine and going and chasing after the one. The laws that are being passed do not empower the one, it only empowers the influential, which are the ninety-nine percent. The fiber of our country should be to empower the weak, so they can become strong. Not to empower the strong so the weak can become weaker. Is it a wonder why there is such an imbalance of equality in this country?

Americans are becoming more like deer every day because they are only becoming good for prey. The powers that be are making sure that if there will be reproduction, it will only be reproduction of prey that is weak, not lions that are developed, trained, skilled and command respect. I am an American myself that has benefitted from being a citizen in this country. That will accommodate for the day, but no insight to the problems it has caused and will continue to create. Please do not get me wrong, I absolutely love my country but when it is time to slice up the pie, there is quite a few people who do not usually get their piece or maybe they just get crumbs.

There are new laws that need to be implemented in this country. Then there are old laws that need to be done away with. This is a task they we as a people need to sprint toward. Laws are one of the most important things in our society. Laws work for or against the people of the land. It is all according to what is believed. The law is what shapes our thinking. It is what determines our decision making. When laws are put in place, we do not have to make decisions. The law will decide for us.

The law is what shapes our culture, lifestyle, occupation, etc. Just imagine, the town that I reside in, if I decided to start a petition, I would need a certain number of signatures.

The signatures will show whoever the government official is, that in my town I am not the only one who feels this way about whatever the issues are that we are trying to address. Once I have those signatures, I can then submit them to government officials. They decide if the request should be denied or approved. For example, let us just say that this request is approved, and they make it a law.

What happens now is it shapes the people thinking into believing in a concept or way of living that they do not necessarily agree with. If it is a law that is against what others believe it may provoke them to try to come against the law or live somewhere else where that law does not exist in their town. This is what causes many people to migrate toward another town or away from another region where the law is more of a reflection of their belief system.

GET TO IT QUICKLY

One day my neighbor came over and knocked on my door and said to me, "There is a lot of water running from the front of your house out into the street."

So immediately I ran outside to take a look to see what he was talking about. The water was spilling into the street from my lawn. I quickly went to the main switch and cut the water off to stop the gushing water and to prevent from incurring a high-water bill.

I called the water company to come out and take a look to see where the leak was located. This was an emergency situation as far as I was concerned, but the water company did not see it this way. Maybe that's because water bill was not their responsibility. They took a day and half to come and fix the busted pipe that caused all the running water. I was very annoyed that they took their time coming to our rescue. I was so relieved the pipe that busted was on the side of the city which made them responsible, and it did not cost me anything.

They did not see the situation as I did, I wanted them to sprint to it. I am sure there are things in your life where you need to sprint? What are the things that you need to sprint to and can't be put to the side any longer?

There are a couple of blank pages at the back of this book. Please write this down and then add your answers:

1. LIST 5 THINGS IN YOUR LIFE WHERE YOU MUST SPRINT TOWARD.
2. LIST 5 THINGS IN YOUR LIFE THAT YOU NEED TO SPRINT AWAY FROM.

UNDERSTANDING YOUR EVENT

The sprints in life can be vastly different from the sprints on a track and field. Life sprints occur too often because of neglect, abandonment, procrastination, and simply just the lack of effort. I will take a hard worker any day over a skilled, talented, gifted, but lazy person any day of the week. Do not get me wrong, I'd rather take the skilled, talented, gifted, and hardworking individual, but through my life experience I have learned that those assets don't normally live in the same body. I find that it is exceedingly rare.

I have seen it to be too common that skilled, talented, gifted people very seldom practice or study. I know that there are always exceptions to the rule. What a select few are able to do with extraordinarily little effort, others can practice all day long and still not measure up is baffling. If you can be the best without rehearsing, is there a need to rehearse? This is the place where the gifted, skilled and talent say I can walk but you probably need to sprint. I believe many geniuses could have been born if it were not for so many people telling them how smart they were.

Being born into lack has given many an advantage because it birthed out tremendous drive for many. Just as sometimes being born privileged gave an abortion to drive, because other people were driving for them.

In life, sprinting has become all too common place, it seems that the lack of preparation has put us at a great disadvantage. I once lived in the zone of hurry up as well. All because of my ability to sprint in most situations. I tried doing everything fast.

I also expected fast results. I did not control the clock, it controlled me, it became the ruler of my life and I was a slave to it. As you may have guessed, as a result I really did not enjoy my days or my life for that matter.

I always felt overwhelmed and overextended. There was never enough time in a day. This is the time I discovered that I needed to sprint toward time management and live in the realm of planning. I had to accept the fact I could not sprint all the time.

The event did not always require speed, sometimes it was observation, other times it was concentration, sometimes everything but speed.

Have you ever gone through a drive-thru and there were so many cars that you wanted to go somewhere else? But you were so hungry and tired that you decided to wait? We probably all have. I remember this very thing happened to me. There were about twelve cars in the drive-thru in front of me and I figured I was in for a long wait.

To my surprise, I was receiving my food within four minutes. I was so happy until I looked in my bag and my burger and fries were cold. It was not the quality food I was expecting to get. I took the food and asked the restaurant to refund my money because I was very dissatisfied. This is great example of knowing when to apply speed. This company was consumed by customer service but not customer satisfaction. They were right to assume that any customer would rather have their food quickly but not at the cost of quality and freshness.

There was a sandwich shop in my hometown of Chicago. The restaurant made arguably the best sandwiches in the entire Chicagoland area. The restaurant was always packed and full to its capacity. If their sandwiches could have been graded by the public, it would have been an A+ across the board. Notice I said the sandwiches and not the service. The service was terrible, and terrible is a feeble word to really describe how bad it was. People would call in their orders to try to avoid the long wait periods.

No matter what creative ways customers tried to improve their experience, it would always fail. The customer service was horrific, but the sandwiches were something you would never forget if you had one.

The operation was a marathon experience when it should have been a sprint. Whatever your role in is in life, you must embrace it to get the outcome you want. Whether you are single, married, a mother or father, an athlete, employer, employee, or entrepreneur, do not shy away from your role - embrace it!

CHAPTER 3

The Marathon

We are living in a society where everything is increased for speed and accuracy. Whether it be computers, cell phones, vehicles, electronic devices, you name it, doing things quickly is a must if you are going to be a competitor in any arena. Especially in the business world. Whether it is being a leader in business, service, product, power, efficiency or what have you, best believe the secret sauce of the majority, of every company -- is the ingredient of hurry up. If we are to be honest, a marathon sounds quite boring. It lacks so much appeal just because of the world of speed that we dwell in for everyday necessities. For example, traffic it such a nuisance for us all because we are not being condition to wait for things anymore.

We now have a drive-thru for almost everything. It is a supreme insult for us to be inconvenienced even for a short period of time. The word wait has become profanity.

The marathon is unattractive, undesirable, it is not appealing or colorful to say the least. It is dull. Often, marathons are frowned upon because most of us want to accomplish things as quickly as possible. When we think of the word marathon the first thing that normally comes to one's mind is time. This is going to take a lot of time to do. Can you remember any celebrated marathon winners? To my recollection there is no one I remember on the Wheaties cereal box or beverage commercials that won any marathons. That is not to say they do not exist.

I have noticed that it is not common that one individual is celebrated for being the first one to cross the line in a marathon. Although they may receive some recognition for being the winner in this race.

But anyone who participates, and finishes, is already deemed as a winner in a marathon.

In the marathon you must be methodical, calculated, planned, meticulous, meditated, studied, thoughtful and very well put together.

I love the marathon because I consider it to be the most important race of all. It is not like the 100-, 200-, or 400-meter races, it is in a category all by itself.

This race is the only race where everyone can be a winner. In the marathon you are not concerned about who is behind or who is in front.

The whole purpose of the race is for everyone to finish. Just imagine what you could accomplish if you could take your time and not worry about who is behind or who is in front of you. I already know that you envision yourself taking the world by storm.

If you have ever noticed, no television network shows a marathon in its entirety because no one knows how long it will take. However, they will show the start of the race and the finish of the race.

It has been determined that these are the most important parts to be seen. But the in between of the start and finish is the most significant aspect of the race.

I have a distinct perspective when it comes to the marathon because the start and the finish is not the race, but the race is the in between. For example, the day you were born and the day that you die are not your life. Your life is the *in between*. The in between part is the real race. Everything that happens in the in between is what matters. Too often we are shown what people did which is the start and the finish of the race. The in between is the how someone was able to finish the race. My objective is to explore the *in between of the race.*

The marathon can include everyone, but it is not for everyone. It is for the mature, patient, persevering, hopeful, and the visionary. It is for the one who can be satisfied without seeing success immediately, but understands it is going to take a bit of time.

When I was younger. I believed and thought wearing glasses was the worst thing that could happen to a person. Growing up wearing glasses was not as fashionable as it is now. There was always someone who would call you unfavorable names because you had to wear them.

The improvement of eye wear has literally gone from zero to one hundred. Glasses have become so fashionable that people who do not even need glasses wear them because they believe they look good in them. I have friends and family that would wear glasses, and the child's understanding I had was that they had to wear them all the time. It did not seem like they ever got any breaks or days off from wearing them. One day someone explained the difference to me about people wearing glasses and what their needs were, rather they were near sighted or far sighted.

I never knew there was such a thing because I did not wear glasses and never had a need to be diagnosed. Then, it was explained to me that if you were nearsighted, you could not see things clearly unless they were relatively close.

But, if you have farsighted, you can see things clearing that are far away but not as clear if they are in close vicinity. This information was a great revelation for me at the time because I began to understand even though I had not been wearing physical glasses that I was nearsighted. I did a self-examination, not on my eyes but on my vision.

There was a time I was not able to see myself as being successful without looking outside of my present circumstances. I was only able to see me progressing right where I was instead of where I could be. When you are nearsighted, you put limitations on your thinking as well as your potential. But being farsighted causes the things that are close to be clouded but your future is clear and as bright as the sun.

Then questions began to arise in me. Did I see myself going really far in my life, or did I see myself staying in the same place and not growing, merely being subjected to my surroundings?

While most people would look at the marathon as being just a race you physically run, they are partially right, but it is so much more.

The marathon is actually a mindset, it is a way of thinking. It is the type of thinking that is inclusive and wants everyone to win. This is not commonly looked at enough in our society as an objective. Do you think in the marathon mindset? I know you are saying what is the marathon mindset? I would like to give you three mindsets.

The run mindset, the sprint mindset, and the marathon mindset. You have been reading about the first two. The run mindset is - I am a competitor and I need to hurry so I can qualify, I want to be like everyone else. The sprint mindset is - I need to beat all the competitors so I can be the winner and set myself apart from everyone else. The marathon mindset is not only do I want to win but I want everyone else to win and finish the race. These mindsets are not one better than the other, it is a matter of placing them in their proper perspective at the appropriate times in our lives.

I have never run a physical marathon, but I have run for great distances for long periods of time. There were plenty of times while running that my body was being carried by my mind and then it switched.

My mind was being carried by my body, then my body and mind began to align with one another and determined when it was time to stop.

The beauty of a marathon is that you can stop and start again. I look at the marathon as being legacy, generational. I can pick up the race that someone else started and begin where they left off. My job is to run and leave behind greatness that can be easily patterned and applied.

Some of us may have to start the marathon because those before us never began. This gives light to why many of us started so far behind in the race from everyone else. It is not about how fast you start nor is about how long it takes, but it is about what you leave behind. What you leave behind has more significance than what was left behind for you. It is the true measurement of how successful you were. That is why I feel so blessed in my life, not because I have so much money or all the riches of the world yet. I have four sons and two daughters that will pick up this race and continue it to a greater place.

There are so many causes in the world that need our support. I find it interesting when people are trying to raise money whether it is to fight cancer, aids, or another struggle, they generally use marathons to support their cause. Just as I said previously, the marathon is a race where everyone can participate, and everyone can be a winner just by finishing. Everyone can make and give a contribution.

In life we are taught to go and live a productive and successful life, but this can be very confusing to many because how do you go and live a successful life when you do not even know how to have a successful day. If you cannot tell time, you should not go and buy a watch. Or you need to learn to tell time. I think a long life can be miserable if you do not even know how to have a successful day. Our world is full of people who have seemingly desirable lives that they do not enjoy.

What our world has recognized as the elite and so-called celebrities of our day and time are people who deal with a great deal of self-hatred and would like to commit suicide and they sometimes do. Ironically, everyone else seems to love them but they hate themselves. Everyone loved Robin Williams but based on stories told about him by close family and friends, he hated himself and suffered greatly throughout his life, all while being highly celebrated and adored.

No matter how great some people may see you to be, if you do not see that about yourself, you may be nearsighted. I have news for you friend, you need a new prescription. Stop wearing other people glasses. Stop looking at yourself from other people's view of you. Start looking at yourself the way that God sees you.

One day I decided I would run six miles a day because I wanted to get back in shape. My objective was to run three miles going and three miles back. When I started off it was quite a challenge. The first day I began running, I started at a calm pace that I could handle.

My breathing was good, and I was not cramping up so, I remained at a very steady pace. When I reached about a mile and a half, I started telling myself I was doing well.

As I continued to run, there was another jogger who passed me swiftly from behind. I had no idea where he had come from. In my amazement of his speed and seemingly effortless pace, my competitive nature was stirred.

Then I said to myself, "I can't wait to get to that level where I can run like that."

So, I continued to jog and make sure that as I was inspired but not too inspired by the jogger that passed me. Everything in me was saying you can go faster pick up your pace. I resisted the impulsive voice in my head to increase my speed and I remained steady and kept running at the same pace. My competitive nature and pride were trying to take over and make things about others when it was only about me. Competition can be deadly because it can be the pathway that sometime leads to pride. In this scenario it was absolutely the case. We must be careful of competition and pride because it will redirect your focus and cause you to lose your purpose.

As I was approaching my three-mile mark and preparing myself to turn around and finish the last three miles, unexpectedly, here comes another jogger passing me again at a pretty fast pace. I understood I was not there for a competition, but it annoyed me that a couple of guys had passed me. There I was again, just telling myself to remain focused, I am doing well, forget who is passing you. My mind started to shift, and I put my thoughts on the task at hand and before I knew it, about a mile away I could see the finish line.

Running with my head up, I got closer to the finish line. I became excited because the two joggers that had passed me during the race were about less than a hundred feet from me.

What a moment I had just had, learning how to keep my focus on what I am doing. Those other joggers were not competing against me, I was not there for a competition or a race, but I had made it about that.

There are moments that will happen in life when distractions are not so easily detected. I had to remind myself of what my purpose was for running. It was not to keep up with anyone or compare myself to any other. My purpose was to reestablish myself as a runner. Being competitive can be a great distraction because we can become too involved with someone else progress.

Then we begin to measure their status when we do not have the proper information to do so. Even if we had the proper data, it is not our business to be focused on that. Competition in this scenario just serves as an avenue to lead to extreme pride. Competition and pride can cause you to abort your purpose and compare yourself to individuals who you see yourself less than or more than. My focus was to get back in shape.

It was another day, and I was running a few hills that had a great incline. As a result, this became very undesirable because it was hard but a challenge to me. So, I ran the hill anyway but dreading it the entire time. While I was running up the hill, I began to develop a technique. I began to tilt my body slightly forward and keep my head down.

The more I tilted forward and began to crouch my body a little it became easier as I ran. I was empowered with this newfound technique that was working quite well for me. Now every occasion that I am running up a hill, I apply this technique. Tilt my body forward and slightly crouch down. It is sort of like humbling yourself before the mighty hill. Running in an upward position was not smart at all for me. It only made my run much harder.

Taking on a new technique was not only smart but wise. Why do I say this? The course had changed but it was still the same path. Since the course was changing it was vitally important for me to change my posture. The path is designed to take me up, so why am I running in an upward position. In my estimation, I think this is incredibly parallel to life.

We run through life and we are faced with many obstacles, circumstances, hills, valleys, and challenging situations, but it does not so easily occur to us. Maybe I should change my posture, tilt my body forward, or approach this situation differently. The inclines and the declines on those hilly paths were designed to go up and down. Living a righteous life that is committed to Jesus Christ is a path that is designed to take you up. Living an unrighteous life without Jesus Christ is a path that is designed to take you down.

When facing something different, we know it is important to adjust. For example, if you are driving in your car on a hot, sunny day with your air condition running, and listening to the radio, it might unexpectedly begin to rain.

Do you just ignore the rain and keep driving, or do you adjust and turn on your windshield wipers? Of course, you turn on the windshield wipers and keep driving. But in life, many of us are faced with different occurrences and some of us remain the same and do not react.

We do not make the necessary adjustments to create a different outcome. Some paths are designed to take you up and other paths are designed to take you down. Pay close attention to the path that you are choosing to follow.

Successful paths are not always attractive or the most appealing to the eye and mind. More often than not, unsuccessful paths are filled with pleasure and immediate gratification.

These fruitless paths seem to be easily accessible and do not necessitate a concentrated effort to acquire. To the eye of little understanding, the successful path appears as a beautiful car with a tank full a gas that can take you anywhere you would like to go.

To our understanding the successful paths appear as if walking two miles to the bus stop to get on a city bus that will take you where you want to go.

Then waiting there for 30-45 minutes to connect to another bus that will take you east, and then walking two more miles to finally arrive at your destination.

Imagine having to repeat this process five days a week? Success is hard work, there is no other way around it.

NO MAN'S LAND

On various occasions, I have been familiar with what one might call a *yes man.* You know the type, the person who is willing to comply to whatever is being asked of them. The yes man has great value because he is willing to follow the rules and take orders and carry them out as they are given.

The yes man takes on the position of the servant, they make the people they serve great because of their willingness to say yes. I would say by my observation is that this type of man (or woman) is becoming rare in our everyday society. I would even go further to say in society, the yes man is despised and looked upon as naïve.

One might even say that they are being undervalued and will not reach their full potential. There are numerous success stories about people who were willing to give and be the yes man and it served them well. I solute them with great respect.

The yes man explores every opportunity and does not allow anything or anyone to slip away because it could be your moment. As a younger man I was so impressed with the many different things that one could acquire. I saw that it gave you favor with people, the respect of some people, and a presumed status. But as I began to mature, my perspective changed. I was not impressed by the things that people could get. I became more impressed with the things a person could refuse. That caused me to want to become a "*no*" man.

We hear all the time about *yes* men and that is great. I 've grown tired of hearing the cliché story of someone that gained the whole world and lived happily ever after.

I want to hear the story of someone who said *no* to the chance to gain the whole world and lived happily ever after.

The word *yes* sometimes equates to giving up control and allowing someone else to decide for you, while the word *no*, sometimes equates to taking control and deciding for yourself.

The *no man* is someone who is not praised or magnified because of his choices. One of the greatest assets in life in my estimation is the ability to say no. When I say the word no, I am not just talking about the ability to tell other people no, but the ability to say no to yourself.

The denial of self is a powerful tool. Growing up as a young man, I would hear so many stories of men who were able to conquer a woman's interest to feed their own desires. Unfortunately, it is still something that is glorified. The story of the late great basketball hall of famer Wilt Chamberlain said he had been with more than twenty thousand women during his lifetime.

This is my view on this matter, but what would have been more glorious is if Wilt Chamberlin used these opportunities to resist his desires, and some of the women's desires toward him by simply saying no. In this scenario I believe his saying no could have touched twenty thousand women for a lifetime instead of touching twenty thousand women for a moment. What is interesting, one moment can ruin a lifetime, just as a great moment can last a lifetime.

So often we are entrapped by things to which we cannot say no. I believe that every man should arrive at a moment where they live in *"no man's land."* Running life's marathon requires us to be in control throughout the race and our life. As much as I would not mind having the power to change many people's circumstances, or the power to make all sick people well, those powers would not satisfy if I did not possess the ability to say no. There are not any statistics on this matter, at least not that I am aware of, but I am willing to wager that people have more tales of woe from not saying no as opposed to people that have benefited in ways from saying yes.

If you are going to run a marathon, you must possess the ability to say no. There will be many opportunities during a marathon that your body and your mind are going to want to give up. Do not give in to that need.

During a time when faced with adversity and scrutiny, the late entertainer, Michael Jackson, once said that *lies run sprints, while the truth runs marathons*. I believe he was both right and wrong because lies run more marathons than the truth runs sprints. Lies have outlasted and outran the truth in many a race. Lies are usually sitting around with nothing to do but spread. It is quite often presumed as the obvious.

While many of us have heard the truth is starring you right in the face, the majority of the time is simply symbolic. But we all understand the precise meaning of that expression.

However, I believe it is a rarity. What makes the truth so precious is that it is like unto a treasure. Well, it is a treasure. As we all know, treasures must be sought out, they are usually hidden under the muck and mire of life. Treasures are discovered.

The truth has value all by itself, but it becomes a greater value when lies have covered the truth. For example, a lie can be a forest while the truth can be one tree hidden in the forest.

Another day as I was approaching the halfway mark of my daily run, I saw the sign that said, "Champion." It is the path's indicator that lets you know you have reached the halfway mark and it is time to turn around to complete the run.

I really liked that sign because when I would see it, not only did I know I was halfway finished, but it was also a reinforcer that I am a champion. On this particular day, I passed the halfway mark and continued to run farther than I normally would have gone.

As I was running, I started to see new things that were not familiar to me. I stopped immediately and began looking around wondering where I was.

I realized I knew exactly where I was, but why had I gone so much farther this time? All in a moment's time it dawned on me. The big sign that said *Champion* had been removed. That sign had become such a pivot for me, more than I really understood. This can be such a reflection of our lives, we run through life vicariously, sometimes going farther than what we intended to go. There are no boundaries, limitations, or indicators to remind us just how far we should be going. But what is our purpose in going? Signs are very necessary, not only are they necessary but are essential to life.

When I get in my car and go to the grocery store there is no question or doubt in my mind about how to get there or where it is located. I have been there countless of times and it is embedded in mind. I could get there with my eyes closed. But signs are needed as indicators not just to assure us that we can get where we are going, but that we are on the right path.

I can imagine that some may say I do not need any signs if I am not going anywhere. That may be true, but some of us do not consider that we have not been going anywhere not because we do not desire to do so.

It is simply because we do not have signs up. Signs are not just directions, but they are also instructions, too. I have signs posted all over my house, those signs are for instructions, because it reminds me this is what I should be doing daily. Life happens, and it can cause you to lose focus quickly.

The greatest danger in losing focus is that you can stay distracted too long and now you have something else you probably should not be focusing on. But it only became your focus because you stayed distracted for too long. It is scary because the thing that was distracting you is no longer your distraction but now it is your focus. I would like to challenge you, look at your life and determine what is a distraction and what is your focus. If you are easily distracted, you are not getting done the things you should be.

The objective of your distraction is to redirect, slow down, frustrate, get you to thinking you can never accomplish what you set out to do.

It will predict your failure. The goal of your focus will be to inspire, encourage, provoke, and place a demand on your potential. It will be able to predict your success. When God wants to advance you, he will bring someone into your life. When the enemy wants to stop you or keep right where you are, he will bring someone into your life. Our responsibility is to discern, determine, and qualify who should be there and who should be removed. The time comes when we see what works and what does not.

There was an experience I had on my way to the local store one day. This was an unforgettable day due to the accident that occurred. I am not even sure what I was going to the store for, but after what happened I don't remember if it was worth it at all. First, I decided to ride my bike to the store just to get a little exercise. The store was about a mile away from my house. I rode to the store and got what I needed and proceeded to turn around and go back home. As I was riding, I started getting really hot. So, I took off the wind breaker jacket that I was wearing and placed it on my handlebars. The jacket was hanging off the handlebars. As you can imagine, this was a huge mistake. Normally I would never do anything like this knowing the potential hazard. On my way back home, the jacket got completely caught in my front tire. The jacket was so tangled that it caused my wheel to come to an immediate stop and threw me over the handlebars and knocked me unconscious. The accident caused me to hit the concrete pavement face first.

When I came back to consciousness, there was a man standing close to me trying to help me and asked me if I was okay. He said he had seen my bike on the ground and saw me covered in blood and running around in circles, so he gotten out of the car to help.

I was so grateful that he stopped to check on me, but after a while everything started to come back to my memory. I had no idea of where I was or who I was.

Allow me to pause right here because I really want to emphasize this point. The desire of the wicked one is to have us forget our identity or never embrace it.

The greatest weapon he can use against us is to put us or keep us in state of mind that we do not know who we are. It has come to the point where people are functioning like they have dementia. Keep in mind, they have not been medically diagnosed, but display all the symptoms.

According to ALZ.org, the definition of dementia is a general term for loss of memory, language, problem-solving, and thinking abilities that are severe enough to interfere with daily life. So many people are in a state of dementia without a diagnosis.

They do not know if they are coming or going, if they want friends or enemies, if they want to be single or married. They are not sure if they want to be employed or unemployed.

Lacking the ability to make simple but necessary decisions, these people live in the city of doublemindedness, the symptoms are to live your life in a lukewarm state.

They never have to be precise, consistent, steady, or reflect any sort of stability. To live here you must have a propensity to not follow through on things and do everything by being spontaneous, never plan for anything, they feel it is so boring to do things that way.

Anyone can do a self-evaluation for this issue. It is a group of persons or person that is gifted, talented, and always seem to be in the know. They possess a knowledge of almost everything in life. They have skillsets in many avenues of the workforce, but they themselves do not have a job anywhere or at least not for a long period of time. The world has a ridiculously cute name for describing these people. They call them the Jack of All Trades.

These were just a few measuring sticks to see if you fit the criteria for this town. If you do, hurry up and make some necessary adjustments to live in a better atmosphere. The determining factor that a person suffers from dementia is that they cannot decision make, nor can they determine their own identity of themselves or others. There is an entire generation of people who ascribe and embrace this deadly ideology.

It is the ideal of not wanting to be identified because identity requires responsibility. The wicked one knows if he can get us to throw away our identity, our responsibility goes right along with it. If your identity is uncertain then your assignment will not even be discovered. If you reject who you are, you will not have any idea of what you should be doing in life.

The wicked one understands that identity determines behavior. To this day, I am humble by the experience that I had on that bike because I always think of how bad it could have been. In a prior paragraph, I talked about things hanging off you and how much it can hold you back. I hope this story gives credence to that statement.

My jacket had no evil intentions toward me, but it was hanging off the bike that I was riding and almost cost me my life. Beware of things hanging off you and beware of people hanging on to you.

The secrets that I learned from just running were life changing because it helped me bring my life into alignment with my goals.

One of the most common questions that I would get from people was how I could run for so long without stopping? The answer became apparent after a while. Control your pace and breathing is a simplified answer but, sometimes more details can help. On my usual daily jog, I would get fatigued quickly and was concerned why that was.

I initially would attribute it to eating too late once in while or something that I ate or drank that did not digest quickly enough. The reason that I was feeling fatigue is my pace would fluctuate. I would not stay at the same pace while I was running but it was not deliberate and that is why I struggled at times.

While I was running my legs started to feel very heavy, I knew I had to push pass what I was feeling and just keep going. So, I did, and I was able to get through my run without incident. Once I got close to about half a mile from finishing, I started to feel that tiredness again.

I did a quick self-check to make sure my body was in an upright posture, my feet were slightly parted, and my arms were in a cool swing of back and forth. The body is so mechanical that it will produce the results you want, just make sure that the body is in harmony.

My arms were the physical key to finishing my run without stopping. Although, if the arms stop moving, the legs will eventually follow suit. Therefore, I just kept my arms up and my body was put on cruise control. I then knew, I would be able to go just long as I liked and stop whenever I wanted.

After I had this experience, I was able to apply this method every time I would go on my run. Just like an airplane in the air, just as long as the wings stay in an upward position, the plane can finish the journey. Of course, this is providing there are no engine problems.

The arms of the plane controls and guides the aircraft all the way on its mission. If you ever noticed, it is not often will you see someone running with their hands down.

Letting your arms drop is viewed as a sign of defeat, just as raising your arms is a sign of victory. Find out what is the initiator in your life that keeps you on the right track.

The harmony of signals is vitally important because everything is connected to one another. I have a distant relative that is mentally handicapped. I remember when he was about twenty years old the doctor told his mom that his brain was at a two-year-old level. At the time, I had no idea what that really meant, as far as his condition was concerned. Now I understand that your brain is what signals to your body and commands response.

The brain signals to the heart, kidneys, lungs, limbs, everything in the body and commands it to grow. So, if the brain's capacity can only deliver at a two-year-old functionality, it is a great possibility that the organs and limbs will not receive the signals and it will not grow.

Even though a person can age year to year, the mind remaining at a two-year-old capacity will create deformity with either the limbs, the organs, or both. This adds credence to the fact so many people that have deformities do not have long lives. Although, there will always be exceptions.

This is a clear-cut picture of a body that is not in harmony. Let us flip this idea on the other side, suppose the mind is functioning properly and signals are being sent and received to its proper places. For example, a ten-year-old boy's mind is at the correct level and everything in his body corresponds. What if he is introduced to inappropriate language, music, and imagery. All these things will develop the mind beyond what the 10-year-old capacity should be.

If slowing down the mind will create deformities because the signals are not communicating properly to the body, would it be safe to say that speeding up the mind will create deformity also? I can imagine it is so.

Our kids today are running around with thoughts that are accelerating their growth. Some are not in harmony within themselves, it is not a wonder why many young people have such an imbalance in their behavior? They are being exposed to so many inappropriate things that are developing them too quickly in things that should not even be aroused in them. Or they are not being developed at all. They are seeing drug use and alcohol consumption, inappropriate male, female interaction before they even know what it is or why it is.

Protection must be our primary concern for the future of our generations. I am not talking about a protection from horrible and harmful people with malicious intent, which is a given. But a protection of the mind, limited access that does not employ corruption to be at their fingertips.

Not only do the youth of our world need protection from the thieves that can control the canvas of their minds but adults, as well.

Mental health services are highly coveted now and are overcrowded with youth and adults who are not able to control the thoughts that are coming to their mind.

They do not have any defense for the mental attacks that have been launched against them. The common treatment that health care professionals provide as solutions is medication. This just creates chemical dependencies that eventually matures to addiction. When it comes to solutions nowadays, people are not thinking on the lines of the marathon which is what is going last to the test of time.

They are thinking only in terms of the sprint which is, let us just fix it quick and that is not going to solve the problem. The physical make-up of human beings is six dimensional. The front and back, left and right, up and down, and all these dimensions are significant.

The path that I run is in a residential and commercial area where there is always something happening. I pass three intersections while on my run which demand of me to remain alert all times. Starting with my front, I must pay attention to what is coming toward me, and from behind I am concerned about cars and bike riders, making sure that I can prevent incidents and accidents from occurring unnecessarily. Not knowing what is behind you can be such a scary thing because you do not see what is coming. Something can run upon you so quickly before you even know that it is there.

Tigers are known for attacking their prey from behind. The bushmen from colder climates were known for creating masks that they would wear on the back of their heads to make it look like they were always facing the tiger. Of course, this was an attempt to discourage tigers from a potential attack from behind. I believe nothing hurts like that thing that one cannot see coming. Our bodies are not even designed to see a clear-cut view of our back.

No matter how perfectly made a mirror can be, we still do not get the privilege of seeing our backs fully. We are forced to depend on someone else for sight when it comes to our backside. The backside exposes how fragile, needy, and vulnerable we really are as human beings, so we can be wounded without knowing it. This is a confirmation to me that people are made for relationships. Two can be better than one.

Have you ever heard the phrase, "He stabbed me with a soft knife"? A soft knife is a knife you cannot see, it comes from the blind side which is our backs. A soft knife can be more deadly than a real knife. A real knife will cut, tear, scar, and leave a wound and shortly thereafter you can be stitched, cleaned, and bandaged up.

But the soft knives are *deadly words* that tear and create wounds that can never be healed nor stitched up because these cutting words stay with you.

The pain of the soft knives is not what does the most damage, but the discovery of who you trusted to protect you and did not is where the pain begins. That is because the wounds come from unexpected places and people. Metaphorically speaking, we have all heard it said quite often that we need watch our backs, but we cannot. Since we do not have the ability to watch our own backs, make sure you are picking the right people to be in relationships with, whether they are work or personal.

The up and down dimension is fairly easy and simplistic. If it is sunny, I look for the shady spots while running, if its cloudy, I have to make sure I will not be caught in the rain for the distance I run. Looking down is something I must do quickly as possible, although I must be incredibly careful while doing it. I do not look down for too long because it can be hazardous to your run for obvious reasons. The word finish represents two outcomes that are attached to its meaning. One is that a task has been completed and there is a victory and the other is a task completed before you could add your contribution, but it is a loss.

Finishing does not come easily, even when there is preparation applied. The work must be done when it comes to the marathon. I run every day and let me tell you, when I get closer to the end it becomes a challenge most of the time. I cannot say if its mental, physical, or what? My experiences have taught me that finishing is hard.

In my experience, people have started in the educational system whether it is high school, college, medical school, law school, and the list goes on. When it is time to graduate, there is only about a third of the people left who started from the beginning. The numbers take a huge dive because finishing is not easy. We all know that education is a marathon, not a sprint.

There must be a commitment. Most of us can do quite a few things and do them well, just as long as we do not have to commit. Having fun usually does not require a commitment because fun is usually adorned with minimal effort. Although, there are quite a few people who work so hard that they do not know how to have fun. A true worker finds fun in completing task continually.

I remember hearing a story of a married couple who was married for ten years and had five children. The couple started off well as most couples do. After about a decade or so they began to have problems and the relationship became tensed, so the husband decided to leave and just move on with his life, and he did. He left his wife and five children and began on another journey.

He moved to another state, found employment, and within a couple of years he bought a house and started another family with a new woman, and they had two children.

They lived as a typical family who did normal day to day things and spent time with one another. After about twenty-five years the man died with two businesses, multiple properties he owned and had a net worth to the tune of about five million dollars. His loved ones were devastated at his passing as expected. The mother of his two children was not his wife, she was just a lifetime partner.

The businessman's wife with whom he had the five children, never heard from him since the time he left twenty something years ago. The wife and his kids inherited all of her husband's businesses and properties. The woman whom he lived with was not entitled to his inheritance, only her children were.

The businessman never got a divorce from his wife. He ran a marathon for more than twenty-five years with his two additional kids and their mother, but he never did finish. Imagine from the story I just shared the negative impact this man had on these people's life. He never finished the marathon.

Everybody starts but only a few seem to finish. Look into your own life and think about if there are people, situations, and circumstances that you walked away from and never finished.

Does your family have the answers they need from you to unlock the paths that they will one day journey through? Or will your life of incompletions be stumbling stones in their lives?

A good father will not leave you with questions he will only leave you with answers, and a path to pick up and continue your own journey.

The things we desire in life will eventually bring us to the valley of decision. The time comes when we all must choose the weapon we are going to fight with. That also means leaving other options on the table that could be potentially beneficial. Sacrifice is what will always be required at some point.

When we take a hold of something, keep in mind other things might be getting away. That is not necessarily a bad thing, but it should provoke the thought that what we are willing to hold on should be worth the risk. All choices are loaded with risk. We are putting at risk winning or losing. One has got to happen and certainly both will happen during the journey. The thing we should not be willing to risk is choosing. Never put yourself in circumstances where you have forfeited the power of choosing and others are empowered to choose for you.

Decide within you if you will live your life as the run, the sprint, or the marathon. True wealth is having the power to choose. While lack of vision can be equated to having someone choose for you. Move cautiously when choosing the run, the sprint, or the marathon. Let's Go!

Lightning Source UK Ltd.
Milton Keynes UK
UKHW010755110821
388656UK00001B/12

9 780578 964850